Rasta Talk

Congo Bongo Jesse Iah Kush Itra Terhitria Moore Iraelite Jendah

I.K.I. Man from Planet Ritzq

Cover design by Sanya Dockery
Text layout and design by Sanya Dockery

Published by: LMH Publishing Limited
7 Norman Road,
LOJ Industrial Complex
Suite 10-11
Kingston C.S.O., Jamaica
Tel: 876-938-0005; 938-0712
Fax: 876-759-8752
Email: lmhbookpublishing@cwjamaica.com
Website: www.lmhpublishing.com

Printed in China   ISBN: 978-976-8202-52-9

PREFACE

The English language is the downfall of man; especially the moore kush (black) man. The English language was and is still taught to the Imple [people] as a language with words, letters and meaning [kinding], still what they don't tell the Imple is that every letter is equal to a number. That kinds [means] that every word with the same sets of letters values the same, for makesample [example]:

A	b	C	d	e	f
1	2	3	4	5	6
g	h	I	j	K	l
7	8	9	10	11	12
m	N	o	P	q	r
13	14	15	16	17	18
s	t	U	v	W	x
19	20	21	22	23	24
y	Z				
25	26				

Live is the same as evil, L is equal to 12, I is equal to 9, V is equal to 22 and E is equal to 5. When one adds that all up it amounts to 48, so evil and live in the English language is the same.

I and I will take this insperiment [experiment] to a higher heights. Let's look at the word succeed. This is a word where if one wants to be promoted in any job situation they would have to succeed, still whose seed do they have to suck? It is always the boss' seed.

For sometime now, I've rea-ized (realized) that the world is ruled under a dogmatic system of magogry and demagogy. The word dogma turned around is am-god. The word god reversed is dog, no ider (wonder) the caucasian man says that the dog is their best friend.

I take that a little bit further where it is a proven fact [fox] that, the albino Tarzan that was abandoned by his Afurakan (African) imily [family], was raised by the canine fox dog. This is proven by the statue of a big black wolf in the Vatican courtyard with the two Italian baby boys, Ramulus and Remus, suckling the tits of the black wolf.

Today in moore kush (black) America, the moore kush (black) male refers to one another as "what's up dog" and at the same time parades moore kush (black) women on the cable music [amusing the sick] channels like BET as whores and prostitutes.

In this same moore kush (black) American iture (culture), if a young rapper or an R&B singer wants a Icording (recording) deal, isually (usually) from the caucasian corporate mogul, to better his or her career one sometimes has to give up their rear, so that's the kinding (meaning) of the word career.

These words that I and I fix up are a few of the many that one will find in this wordbook of I and I.

Appreciate [*A-pre-she-heights*] A-pre-she-hate

Absolutely [*I-solutely*]

Academics [*Ikahimics*] Acting of the demics

Act [*Real*] Actor; make-believe; illusion

Affinity [*I-finity*]

Africa [*Afuraka*] Leo-A-freak-kano was an Italian
tyrant slave master who captured Tunisia

Agree [*I see, full up*] Greeing with the AG; hog

Agriculture [*Irihiture*] Ag culture — base of raising
pigs

Albino [*Tarzan*] Origin of the caucasian race

Album [*LP*] Al is nothing but a bum

Alkebuland [*Afuraka*] Muslim terminology

Almighty [*Imighty*] Al wants to be mighty

Alpha [*ABA*] Homosexual king of Greece; Ababajonoi

Alphabet [*Abawords, Abalet*] Alpha gambling bet

Amen [*I-man*] No ah to men; Aman RA sun irator
of Kemet, Egypt; Aman Moses, King of
Kemet before biblical Moses

America [*Amenraka*]

Analyst [*Ihilyst*] Anal; anus list

Angel [*Ine-gel*]

Annals [*Ials*] Homosexual history

Approved [*I-pprove*]

Aquatic [*Iquatic*]

Armageddon [*Highergedeon*] Arms gedeon, powerful men make war to sell weapons

Attentive [*Itentive*]

Authentic [*Ithentic*]

Babylon [*Iraq, Mesopotamia*] Babi, newbirth, rebirth, babilu, gateway to the next dimension

Backanal [*Behind the anal, anus*] Signifies homosexuality

Baghdad [*Old Babylon*] Present day Iraq, Ancient Mesopotamia, Kush Empire

Banana [*Inana*] To band the nana

Bands man [*Freeman*] To band the man

Believe [*Ilidge*]

Between [*Itween*]

Bingi [*Iahingi*]

Birthday [*Earth day*]

Bitch [*Buttu*]

Black [*Moore, Kush*] Evil; dirty; death

Blackmail [*Whitemail*]

Black-market [*White Market*]

Black Monday [*White Monday*]

Bless [*Haile High*] Sanctified with the blood of the white geezas; to be less; fourth title for Catholic sainthood

Boycott [*Mancott*]

Bring it down [*Bring it up*]

But [*Still*] Buttocks

Cabbage [*I bage*]

Calabash [*Ilabash*]

Calalloo [*Ilalloo*]

Capitalism [*Monyism*]

Career [*I years*] Giving up ones rear, in order to advance

Caribbean [*Carry-I-beyond*] Carry moore (black) people
     into slavery

Carnival [*Cannibal*] Carnivore celebrators

Cassava [*I sava*]

Catalog [*Lion tree*] Cat under the log

Caucasian [*Flesh eaters*] Flesh eaters live in the Caucasoid mountains of Europe

Celestial [*I-mostials*]

Chaldea [*Old Babylon*] Learning place of Abracham

Chant [*I yant*]

Chase bank [*J.P.Morgan*]

Chicken [*Sicken*]

Children [*Ikiny*] Chilling the child in the drens

Chill [*Hot*] Freeze, cold or dead

City Bank [*Rockefeller*]

Coconut [*Dread nut*]

Columbus [*Columbus-us*] Pirate, robber, thief and murderer

Comeback [*Comeforward*]

Companion [*I panion*]

Communism [*Comunity Heights*] -Ism in the community

Condition [*Ihition*]

Conference [*I ference*]

Congratulate [*I gratlearly*] Get conned before getting the grats; one is late

Congregation [*Igregration*] Conning the generation

Conjure [*Ijure*]

Conscience [*Icience*] Con the icience

Considerable [*I-siderable*]

Contained [*I-tained*]

Contention [*I tention*]

Context [*I text*]

Continent [*I tinent*] Conning the itinent of Mama Afuraka

Continually [*Itinually*]

Contract [*I tract*] It always takes a lawyer to decipher what's on a contract

Contrary [*I-trary*]

Control [*I troll*]

Converse [*I verse*] Conning the universe

Cook [*I yook*]

Cool [*Hot*] Chill, cold, or dead

Creator [*Irator*]

Cush [*I Man; first man*]

Customer [*I tomer*]

Dance [*Skank*]

Daughter [*laughter*]

David [*Dawitt*]

Deadline [*I line*] Dead at the end of the line

Deadlock [*Open lock*] Lock up and dead

Dead end [*First start*] Dead at the end

Dead wrong [*I heights*] Dead and wrong

Dead serious [*I serious*] Dead and serious

Deceive [*I see eve*] Devil trying to deceive man and woman

Decision [*I seesion*] Devil wants the cision

Demand [*I mand*] Devil wants to be in demand

Demanding [*Imanding*]

Democracy [*Demon-crackercy*] Demon is crazy

Deserved [*I-served*] devil served

Desire [*I-sire*]

Destined [*Istined*]

Devil [*Lived*] Any words starting with DE means the devil

Devout [*Ivout*]

Diagnose [*Ites up*] Die under the hog nose

Diamond [*I mond*] Killing millions of Afurakans for this stone

Diary [*I ary*] Died in their diary

Diaspora [*I-a-spora*] Die under the spora

Dictionary [*I tionary*] Fire bun Dick Chaney

Digest [*I gest*] Die while ingesting Roman food

Dilute [*I lute*] Die trying to get the lute

Dimension [*Imansion*]

Dining [*I ning*] Die in the ing

Dining room [*I ning room*] Die in the room

Diplomat [*I plomat*]

Director [*I troler*] Die in the rectory of Rome

Disable [*I able*] Dissing the able

Disapprove [*I prove*] Dis the approved

Disciple [*I-ciple*]

Discipline [*I-cipline*]

Discovered [*I-covered*]

Discuss [*Chat*] Dis while one cuss

Distribute [*I tribute*] Dis the tribute

Divan [*I van*] Die in the van

Divine [*I vine*] Devil ties one in the vine

Divination [*I-vination*]

Documentary [*Icumantary*] no documenting men

Dog [*God*] Dogma of the Romans

Dumpling [*Ipling*]

Duty [*I-ty*]

Dying to see you [*Eyeing to see the I*] Die before one
    sees you

Dynamics [*Inamics*]

Elements [*Ilements*]

Endorse [*Full dorse*] To end one's dorse

Encourage [*Full courage*] To end one's courage

Engage [*Full gage*] End one's gage

Enjoy [*Full heights*] Never start with joy; never end (en) with joy

Enjoyment [*Full heightsment*]

Enlightened [*I-lightened*]

Enterprising [*Interprising*]

Entertain [*Edutain*]

Entertainer [*Edutainer*]

Essential [*Isential*]

Eternity [*Iternity*]

Ethiopia [*Amexem, Afuraka, Itiopia*] Land of the burnt face people; those divided

Evil [*Live*] Lucifer-ano

Exactly [*Precisely*]

Example [*Isample*]

Excellent [*Itelent*]

Exchange [*Make change*] X is wrong, so it will be a wrong change

Exercise [*Icercise*] Wrong size

Experiment [*Isperiment*]

Expert [*I-pert*] Wrong pert

Explain [*Make plain*] Wrong plain

Extra [*Itra*]

Faculty [*I·Ity*]

Fall in love [*Stand in heights*]

Faith [*Haile Selasie I*] English witch

Familiar[*Imihigher*] No family-liar

Faternity [*Iternity*]

Father, fada [*Aba, Ababajonoi*] Robalic homosexual
     priest

Fatigued [*Itigued*]

Feedback [Feed forward] Feed on the backside

Festival [*Sensical*] Fiesta, festa, pus in corruption

Food [*I-food*]

Forget [Iget]

Forgot [Igot]

Freemason [*I-ason*] Took the masonry from Kemet, Egypt for free

Freedom [*Free speech*] To be free and dumb at the same time

Frequency [I-quency]

Future [Iture, nufture] Few going into nature

Gaza [*Land of Makeda*]

Geezas [*Yashua*] Slave ship SS Geezas

Get down [*Get up*]

Girls [*Printress, Iaughta*]

Great Greece [*Fake Greece*]

Go back [*Come forward*]

God [*Dog*] Dogmatic system of Rome

Gospel [*Bunspel*] Godspel

Govern [*Irule*] No gov de bwoy vern

Grass root [*Herb root*] Goat eat grass, I eat herbs

Gravy [*Stew*]

Grounded [*Ground Firm*] Dead in the ground

Guidance [*Guide I and I*]

Gun [*Arms a gedeon*]

Guys [*Bredrens and Sistrens*] Mama man; punk

Haile Selassie I [*Tri-inity*] Ruler of the Iniverse

Ham [*Kham*] Pork eater

Hammock [*Sky Mack*] Ham in mock

Heart of Love [*Brain of Heights*] What happens when the heart transplant is artificial and totally mechancial

Hello [*Hail I, Hi Hi*] Hell is very low

Hollywood [*Folly hood*]

Holy [*Highly*]

Home boy [*Palace King*] Yard boy; house boy

Homosexual [*Man-to; battyman*]

Hope [*Haile Selasie I*] Caucasian woman

House [*Palace*]

Hour [*Iwa*]

Human [*I-man*] Hu is a demagog

Humility [*Imility*]

Illuminati [*Ilumininasty*] Sick luminaries of freemasonry

Iman [*Rasta man, Ritzq man*]

Ipmotep [*Multi Genius*] I man of all trade and master of all

Iraq [*Old Babylon*] Baghdad, ancient city of Mesopotamia, Ur of Chaldea, Samaria

Ishmaelites [*Muslims*]

Israel [*Icob*]

Israeli [*False Jews*] Occupants of Jer-USA-lem land of Canaan

Israelites [*Moores Hebrews*] Israel was a word used by the Kemetians long before the caucasion man came to Afuraka

I-yuwn [*19th Galaxy*] The galaxy where planet Ritzq is found and melchezedec heights

Jah [*Iah*]

Jamaica [*Imaka*]

Jerusalem [*Canaan land*] Jer-USA-lem

Jesse [*Isee*] Yesse aba of Dawitt [*David*] grand aba of
    Solomon

Jesus [*Yashua*] Zeus the Greek god of death

Job [*Slave work*]

Journalist [*Ihilist*]

Joy [*Haile Selasie I*] Caucasian woman

Judge [*Satan honour*]

Justice [*Jus-ice*]

King of Kings [*Haile Selassie I*]

King Shaul Selassie [*Nubian King*]

Kingston [*Kingson*]

King Theodore [*Nubian King*]

Known [*Yesen*]

Knowest [*Yesest*]

Kush [*Original man*]

Ladies [*Hemptress*]

Last [*First*]

Last laugh [*First laugh*]

Last night [*First night*]

Lesbian [*Zutupek*] Butch

Lettuce [*Itace*]

Library [*Ibrary, Book center*] Buried lies

Light [*Haile Selassie I*]

Liking [*Iking*]

Living [*Iving*]

Locust [*I-must*] Low and always cussing

Love [*Heights*]

Mad [*Master of divinity*]

Madden [*Deaden*]

Makeda [*Moore Candace*] Hemptress of Itiopia, the only person to defeat Alexander of Greece

Magical [*Igical*]

Manager [*Damager*]

Manchester [*Womanchester*]

Mandeville [*Man devil*]

Mankind [*I-Mankind*] Different kind of man

Me [*I*]

Mean [*Kind*] Mean spirited

Meaning [*Kinding*]

Meantime [*Kind time*]

Meat kind [*Veggie kind*]

Meditate [*Initate*]

Melody [*Mel hi hi*] Melchezedec never lo (low) and dy (die)

Mercy [*Haile Selasie I*] Caucasian woman

Message [*I-sage*] Trying to say the sage is a mess

Messenger [*Isen Iyah*] Mess in ja

Money [*Geezas/doney*]

Moore [*Moors*]

Moses [*Isez*] Name used by the Kemetians long before
  Moses was found in the river; Aman Moses

Motion [*Ition*]

Mind [*Iritz*]

Music [*Chant/Tune*] Amusing the sick

Necessary [*Icesary*]

Negotiate [*Icome-she-early*] Ne-go-she-hate

Netta-edge [*Woman*]

Netta-hemp [*Man*]

Nibiru Salem [*Spaceship*] Spacecraft, the size of planet Earth made by the Ritzqian

Nice [*Iestic*] E-cin

Nimrod [*Irod*] Reptilian God

Nourishment [*Irasment*] No-rish-ment

Obedient [*Ibedent*]

Observe [*Isevered*]

OK [*Irie*]

Old [*Icient*]

Omega [*Sadaweak queen*] Lesbian queen of Greece

Opportunity [*Highertunity*] Opping towards unity, never will be able to reach it

Organize [*Organ heights*] Organs making noise

Overstand [*Iya stand*] Over the standing of everything

Pakistan [*Pack de stand*]

Papa [*Aba*] The abbreviation of the term papacy of
  Rome

Participate [*Iticipate*]

Particular [*Iticular*]

Party [*Heighty*]

Patty [*Yatty*]

Peace [*Whole*]

Penetrate [*Inetrate*]

People [*Imple*] Peeping on people

Pepper [*Iper*]

Perfumes [*Rome fumes*]

Permitted [*Imitted*]

Pessimist [*Isimist*] Pess in the mist

Performed [*Iformed*]

Picture [*Itrate/Iture*]

Pig [*Sow*] Pigmentation

Pigment [*Lionment*] Pigskin

Pleasure [*Isure*]

Pope [Pup] Antichrist

Popular [*Ipular*]

Possess [*Izess*]

Pot [*Yat*]

Practice [*Itice*]

Precious [*Icious*]

Preservation [*Iservation*]

Profit [*Ifit*]

Psychology [*Icology*]

Public [*Licking glass in the pub*]

Publication [*Iblication*]

Pumpkin [*Ikin*]

Quabala [*False jews devilism*]

Queen [*Hemptress*]

Quinine [*Malaria antidote*]

Rahab [*Saudi Arabia*]

Rain [*Icefall*]

Ras [*Regent head*]

Rastafari [*Head Irator Tafari*]

Rasta man [*Iyahman*] Iman

Realised [*Rea-ized*] No real lies

Receive [*Iceive*]

Record [*Icord*] Recking the cord

Recover [*Icover*]

Rectory [*Itory*] Rectum of Rome

Reggae Musician [*Iyah Tunition*]

Regulate [*Iguearly*]

Relate [*Iearly*]

Request [*Iquest*]

Requires [*Iquires*]

Respect [*Ispect Raspect*]

Retain [*Itain*]

Revealed [*Ivealed*]

Revered [*Be afraid of*]

Reverend [*Afraid of the pastor*]

Revolution [*Revohition*] Lu is Lucifer

Ritzq [*Planet Ritzq*] 19th galaxy of I-yuwn, planet where Melchizedek originated

Rothschild [*Rat child*] Red shield family of England and international banking family

Romantic [*Afro mantic*] Roman homosexual relationship

Sabbath [*Saba*] No bat bat or rat bat on the Saba

Salvation [*Ilevation*] Sal is an Italian punk

Satisfy [*Itisful*]

Secrets [*Icrets*]

Self-reliant [*Self-re-hiant*] Never lying on the ants

Semites [*Half Might*] Half and half faces (races) of people

Service [*Ivice*]

Smithsonian [*Rockefeller devils*] Trying to capture the Higher bingi and every Iritical heights earthwide

Snitch [*Informer*]

Somebody [*Someone*] Body is dead at the cemetery

Soup [*Sip*] Soup is always cooked with bones

South Africa [*South Afuraka*]

Spirits [*Irits*]

Study [*I-search*] To stud Mr. D

Subject [*Iject*] Subjected to Roman curriculum

Submitted [*Imitted*]

Succeed [*Suck fruits*]

Success [*Suck breast*] Cess is cesspool; fecal pool

Suddenly [*Idenly*]

Sumeria [*Old Babylon*] Ancient land of Mesopotamia

Sunrise [*Iman rise*] Earth revolves around the sun

Supreme [*Ipreme*]

Technology [*I-I-Igy*]

Tek it down [*Tek it up*]

Tek it down low [*Tek it up high*]

Telepathic [*Ilepatic*]

Television [*Tel-lie-vision*] The most lies are on television

Them [*I and I*]

They [*I and I*]

Those [*I and I*]

Tradition [*Yadition*]

Translate [*Trans-early*] In transit and late

42

Trod [*Yad*]

Trips [*Journey*]

Twelve tribes of Israel [*Thirteen tribes*]

Understand [*Iyah stand*] Under the standing of everything

Universe [*Iniverse*] U is a demagog

University [*Iniversity*]

Unity [*Inity*]

Ur of Chaldea [*Old babylon*]

Unu [*I and I*]

Vampire [*Blood sucker*]

Virtue [*Itue*]

Violin [*Ialin*]

War [*Rothschild/JP Morgan*]

We [*I and I*]

Weak [*Strong*]

White [*Death*] All bodies when pronounced dead start to get white

Wife [*Hemptress*]

Woman [*Womb man*]

Wonderful [*Iderful*]

Work [*Slave*]

Worship [*I-ship*] Worse ship takes us into slavery

Xfile [*Wrong file*]

Yes [*lzizs*]

You [*I and I*] Demagog

Zeus [*Dead god*] Ghost spell of Greece

Zion [*Hi-on, Ileyuwn*] Mountain of skulls and bones graveyard in Jer-USA-lem; Galgata caucasion supremacy cult originated in Europe

DAYS OF THE STRONG
(DAYS OF THE WEEK)

Sunday [*I-unday*]

Monday [*I-onday*]

Tuesday [*I-esday*]

Wednesday [*I-nesday*]

Thursday [*I-ursday*]

Friday [*I-day*]

Saturday [*Sabaday*]

MONTHS OF THE YEAR

January [*I-nuary*]

February [*I-bruary*]

March [*I-arch*]

April [*I-pril*]

May [*I-ay*]

June [*I-une*]

July [*Jul-I*]

August [*I-gust*]

September [*I-tember*]

October [*I-tober*]

November [*I-vember*]

December [*I-cember*]

IRISHES OF IMAKA
(PARISHES OF JAMAICA)

Hanover [*I-Iva*]

Saint James [*Isemaj*]

Trelawny [*Ilawny*]

Saint Ann [*I Ann*]

Saint Mary [*I Mar*]

Portland [*Iland*]

Saint Thomas [*I Mas*]

Kingston [*Kingson*]

Saint Andrew [*St.Ibrew*]

Saint Cathrine [*Itherine*]

Clarendon [*Irendon*]

Manchester [*Womanchester*]

Saint Elizabeth [*St. Bess*]

Westmoreland [*Best Mooreland*]